# THE WISDOM OF
# *LITTLE WOMEN*

# THE WISDOM OF *LITTLE WOMEN*

compiled by Isabel Anders

Text condensed from *Little Women*
by Louisa May Alcott

© 1995 Eggman Publishing, Inc.
All rights reserved. Written permission must be received from the publisher before using or reproducing any portion of this book, other than for the purpose of critical reviews or articles. The proprietary trade dress, including the size and format of this Eggman Publishing, Inc. publication, is the property of Eggman Publishing, Inc. It may not be used or reproduced without the express written permission of Eggman Publishing, Inc.

ISBN: 1-886371-21-0

For interviews and other information:
Eggman Publishing, Inc.
2909 Poston Avenue, Suite 203
Nashville, TN 37203
1-800-396-4626

"Go then, my little book, and show to all
... what ... may be blest
to them for good,
may make them choose to be
pilgrims better, by far, than thee or me. . . .
Let young damsels learn . . .
to prize the world which is to come,
and so be wise . . ."

—from the Preface, adapted from John Bunyan.

# THE JOURNEY

While we wait we may all work, so that these hard days need not be wasted.
    —Father.

Our burdens are here, our road is before us, and the longing for goodness and happiness is the guide that leads us through many troubles and mistakes to the place which is a true Celestial City.
    —Mother.

We have to get by the lions first.
    —Jo.

# FAMILY

Birds in their little nests agree.
>—Beth.

I don't believe fine young ladies enjoy themselves a bit more than we do ...
>—Jo.

Rich or poor, we will keep together and be happy in one another.
>—The Marches.

# GROWING UP

I'll try to be what father loves to call me, a "little woman," and not be rough and wild; but do my

duty here instead of wanting to be somewhere else.
—Jo.

It's proper to use good words and improve your vocabulary.
—Amy.

I wish wearing flatirons on our heads would keep us from growing up. But buds will be roses, and kittens, cats—more's the pity!
—Jo.

# DISCONTENT

When you feel discontented, think over your blessings, and be grateful.
—Mother.

I am happy, and I won't fret; but it does seem as if the more one gets the more one wants, doesn't it?
—Meg.

# CONCEIT

Conceit spoils the finest genius. There is not much danger that real talent or goodness will be overlooked long; even if it is, the consciousness of possessing and using it well should satisfy one, and the great charm of all power is modesty.
—Mother.

It's nice to have accomplishments, and be elegant; but not to show off...
—Amy.

Any more than it's proper to wear all your bonnets and gowns and ribbons at once ...
—Jo.

# HOME

Home is a nice place, though it isn't splendid.
—Meg.

A breath of fresh air seemed to blow through the house and something better than sunshine brightened the quiet rooms. Everything appeared to feel the hopeful change; Beth's bird began to chirp again, and a half-blown rose was discovered on Amy's bush in the window; the fires seemed to burn with unusual cheeriness; and every time the girls met, their pale faces broke into smiles as they

hugged one another, whispering encouragingly, "Mother's coming . . . !"

## ANGER

Don't let the sun go down upon your anger; forgive each other, help each other, and begin again tomorrow.
—Mother.

It's my dreadful temper! I try to cure it; I think I have, and then it breaks out worse than ever. Oh, mother, what shall I do?
—Jo.

Never get tired of trying; and never think it is im-

possible to conquer your fault.
—Mother.

I'm never angry with you. It takes two flints to make a fire: you are as cool and soft as snow.
—Laurie to Amy.

# WORK

You will find that all play and no work is as bad as all work and no play.
—Mother.

Have regular hours for work and play; make each day both useful and pleasant, and prove that you understand the worth of time by employing it well.
—Mother.

# PRAYER

I tried to thank God for being so good to us; but I could only cry, and say, "I'm glad! I'm glad!" Didn't that do as well as a regular prayer? For I felt a great many in my heart.
—Jo.

# MONEY

Money is a needful and precious thing—and, when well used, a noble thing—but I never want you to think it is the first or only prize to strive for. I'd rather see you poor men's wives, if you were happy, beloved, contented, than queens on thrones, without self-respect and peace.
—Mother.

If rank and money come with love and virtue, also, I should accept them gratefully, and enjoy your good fortune; but I know, by experience, how much genuine happiness can be had in a plain little house, where the daily bread is earned, and some privations give sweetness to the few pleasures.
—Mother.

## TROUBLES

What a trying world it is! No sooner do we get out of one trouble than down comes another.
—Jo.

The troubles and temptations of your life are beginning, and may be many; but you can overcome them and outlive them if you learn to feel the

strength and tenderness of your Heavenly Father as you do that of your earthly one. The more you love and trust Him, the nearer you will feel to Him, and the less you will depend on human power and wisdom.
    —Mother.

I bear my troubles well but I do wish Hannah would put more starch in my aprons and have buckwheats every day. Can't she?
    —Amy.

## VANITY

It is nice to be praised and admired; and I can't help saying I like it.
    —Meg.

That is perfectly natural, and quite harmless, if the liking does not become a passion and lead one to do foolish things. Learn to know and value the praise that is worth having...
—Mother.

# SAINTS AND SINNERS

...I wish we could wash from our hearts and souls
    The stains of the week away,
And let water and air by their magic make
    Ourselves as pure as they;
Then on the earth there would be indeed
    A glorious washing day!...
—"Song of the Suds," by Jo.

I can't bear saints; just be a simple, honest, respectable boy...
—Jo.

## GOD

The more you love and trust Him, the nearer you will feel to Him, and the less you will depend on human power and wisdom. His love and care never tire or change, can never be taken from you, but may become the source of lifelong peace, happiness, and strength. Believe this heartily, and go to God with all your little cares, and hopes, and sins, and sorrows, as freely and confidingly as you come to your mother.
—Mother.

# PERFECTION

It's too warm to be particular about one's parts of speech.
—Jo.

I keep turning over new leaves, and spoiling them, as I used to spoil my copybooks; and I make so many beginnings there never will be an end.
—Laurie.

# BURDENS

I've thought a great deal lately about my "bundle of naughties," and being selfish is the largest one in it; so I'm going to try hard to cure it, if I can.
—Amy.

Let me advise you to take up your little burdens again; for though they seem heavy sometimes, they are good for us, and lighten as we learn to carry them. Work is wholesome, and there is plenty for everyone; it keeps us from ennui and mischief, is good for health and spirits, and gives us a sense of power and independence better than money or fashion.

    —Mother.

I want my daughters to be beautiful, accomplished, and good; to be admired, loved and respected; to have a happy youth... and to lead useful, pleasant lives, with as little care and sorrow to try them as God sees fit to send.

    —Mother.

# JOY

I'm so full of happiness that, if father was only here, I couldn't hold one drop more.
 —Beth.

The drop came. Laurie opened the parlor door... "Here's another Christmas present for the March family...." Mr. March became invisible in the embrace of four pair of loving arms.

There never was such a Christmas dinner as they had that day. The fat turkey was a sight to behold, when Hannah served him up, stuffed, browned, and decorated; so was the plum pudding, which quite melted in one's mouth; likewise the jellies, in which Amy reveled like a fly in a honey pot.

# SACRIFICE

A burnt offering has been made of vanity; this hardened palm has earned something better than blisters; and I'm sure the sewing done by these pricked fingers will last a long time, so much good will went into the stitches.
—Father, on Meg's progress.

# FEMININITY

I don't see the "son Jo" whom I left a year ago.... I see a young lady who pins her collar straight, laces her boots neatly, and neither whistles, talks slang, nor lies on the rug as she used to do.... In all Washington I couldn't find anything beautiful enough to be bought with the five and twenty dol-

lars which my good girl sent me.
—Father on Jo's progress and gift.

## PERVERSITY

The best of us have a spice of perversity in us, especially when we are young and in love.

## WORLDLY WISDOM

Your parents, my dear, have no more worldly wisdom than two babies.
—Aunt March.

I'm glad of it.
—Meg.

# GENIUS

It takes people a long time to learn the difference between talent and genius, especially ambitious young men and women.

Amy was learning this distinction through much tribulation, for, mistaking enthusiasm for inspiration, she attempted every branch of art with youthful audacity.

Jo did not think herself a genius by any means; but when the writing fit came on, she gave herself up to it with entire abandon, and led a blissful life, unconscious of want, care or bad weather, while she sat safe and happy in an imaginary world . . .

# SUCCESS

By the magic of a pen, Jo's "rubbish" turned into comforts for them all. "The Duke's Daughter" paid the butcher's bill, "A Phantom Hand" put down a new carpet, and the "Curse of the Coventrys" proved the blessing of the Marches in the way of groceries and gowns.

# WEALTH AND POVERTY

Wealth is certainly a most desirable thing, but poverty has its sunny side, and one of the sweet uses of adversity is the genuine satisfaction which comes from hearty work of head or hand; and to the inspiration of necessity we owe half the wise, beautiful,

and useful blessings of the world.

Poverty enriches those who live above it and is a sure passport to truly hospitable spirits.

## CRITICISM

Criticism is the best test . . . for it will show her both unsuspected merits and faults, and help her to do better next time.
    —Mother on Jo's book.

We are too partial; but the praise and blame of outsiders will prove useful, even if she gets but little money.
    —Mother.

# SCHOOL FOR WIVES

Never deceive him by look or word, Meg, and he will give you the confidence you deserve, the support you need.
    —Mother.

Watch yourself, be the first to ask pardon if you both err, and guard against the little pique, misunderstandings, and hasty words that often pave the way for bitter sorrow and regret.
    —Mother.

# GOOD DEEDS

I wish it was as easy for me to do little things to please people as it is for you. I think of them, but it

takes too much time to do them; so I wait for a chance to confer a great favor, and let the small ones slip; but they tell best in the end, I fancy.
—Jo to Amy.

Women should learn to be agreeable, particularly poor ones; for they have no other way of repaying the kindnesses they receive.
—Amy.

## HONESTY

But I think girls ought to show when they disapprove of young men; and how can they do it except by their manners? Preaching does not do any good, I know ...
—Jo.

# APPRECIATION

It is a pleasure to help people who appreciate our efforts; some do not, and that is trying.
—Aunt March.

# INDEPENDENCE

I don't like favors; they oppress and make me feel like a slave. I'd rather do everything for myself, and be perfectly independent.
—Jo.

# TURNING THE OTHER CHEEK

A kiss for a blow is always best, though it's not very easy to give it sometimes.
> —Mother, with the air of one who had learned the difference between preaching and practicing.

"Thou shalt love thy neighbor as thyself."

I ought, but I don't.
> —Amy.

# WORTHINESS

You've a deal more principle and generosity and nobleness of character than I ever gave you credit for,

Amy. You've behaved sweetly, and I respect you with all my heart.
—Jo.

## PETTINESS

I want to be above the little meannesses and follies and faults that spoil so many women. I'm far from it now, but I do my best, and hope in time to be what mother is.
—Amy.

# OUTSPOKENNESS

Oh, my tongue, my abominable tongue! Why can't I learn to keep it quiet?
>—Jo, remembering words which had been her undoing.

# MIND OVER MATTER

With Jo, brain developed earlier than heart, and she preferred imaginary heroes to real ones, because, when tired of them, the former could be shut up . . . the latter were less manageable.

# DEPENDENCE

Go and make yourself useful, since you are too big to be ornamental. I thought you hated to be tied to a woman's apron string?
—Jo to Laurie.

Ah, that depends on who wears the apron!
—Laurie.

# GENTLENESS

Jo had learned that hearts, like flowers, cannot be rudely handled, but must open naturally.

# MOTHERS

Mothers may differ in their management, but the hope is the same in all—the desire to see their children happy.
—Mother.

What do girls do who haven't any mothers to help them through their troubles?
—Jo.

Mothers have need of sharp eyes and discreet tongues when they have girls to manage.
—Mother.

Mothers are the best lovers in the world.
—Jo.

# LEARNING TO FLY

Jo was eager to be gone, for the home nest was growing too narrow for her restless nature and adventurous spirit.

# POWER

Jo saw that money conferred power; money and power, therefore, she resolved to have; not to be used for herself alone, but for those whom she loved more than self.

The dream of filling home with comforts, giving Beth everything she wanted, from strawberries in winter to an organ in her bedroom; going abroad herself, and always having more than enough, so

that she might indulge in the luxury of charity, had been for years Jo's most cherished castle in the air.

## RIGHT AND WRONG

People want to be amused, not preached at, you know. Morals don't sell nowadays.

Wrongdoing always brings its own punishment; and, when Jo most needed hers, she got it.

Jo valued goodness highly, but she also possessed a most feminine respect for intellect.

# DISILLUSIONMENT

It took Jo some time to recover from the discovery that the great creatures were only men and women after all.

The world was being picked to pieces, and put together on new and, according to the talkers, on infinitely better principles than before. . . . Religion was in a fair way to be reasoned into nothingness, and intellect was to be the only God.

# FAITH

Professor Bhaer was neither rich nor great, young nor handsome . . . He had a hard fight, for the wise men argued well, but he didn't know when he was

beaten, and stood to his colors like a man. Somehow, as he talked, the world got right again to Jo; the old beliefs, that had lasted so long, seemed better than the new; God was not a blind force, and immortality was not a pretty fable, but a blessed fact. She felt as if she had solid ground under her feet again.

## CHARACTER

She began to see that character is a better possession than money, rank, intellect, or beauty, and to feel that if greatness is what a wise man has defined it to be, "truth, reverence, and good will," then her friend Friedrich Bhaer was not only good, but great.

# CONSCIENCE

I almost wish I hadn't any conscience, it's so inconvenient. If I didn't care about doing right and didn't feel uncomfortable when doing wrong, I should get on capitally. I can't help wishing sometimes that father and mother hadn't been so particular about such things.
 —Jo.


# FRIENDSHIP

Well, the winter's gone, and I've written no books, earned no fortune; but I've made a friend worth having and I'll try to keep him all my life.
 —Jo.

# TRUST

Like a confiding child, Beth asked no questions, but left everything to God and nature, Father and mother of us all, feeling sure that they, and they only, could teach and strengthen heart and spirit for life and the life to come.

# PARTNERSHIP

You have only made the mistake that most young wives make—forgotten your duty to your husband in your love for your children. A very natural and forgivable mistake, Meg, but one that had better be remedied before you take to different ways.
    —Mother.

We each do our part alone in many things, but at home we work together, always.
—Mother.

Don't shut yourself up in a bandbox because you are a woman, but understand what is going on, and educate yourself to take your part in the world's work, for it all affects you and yours.
—Mother.

Don't let John be a stranger to the babies, for they will do more to keep him safe and happy in this world of trial and temptation than anything else, and through them you will learn to know and love one another as you should.
—Mother.

# DOMESTIC CONTENT

It was not all Paradise by any means; but everyone was better for the division of labor system; the children throve under the paternal rule ... Meg recovered her spirits and composed her nerves by plenty of wholesome exercise, a little pleasure, and much confidential conversation with her sensible husband. Home grew homelike again, and John had no wish to leave it, unless he took Meg with him.

Meg learned that a woman's happiest kingdom is home, her highest honor the art of ruling it not as a queen, but as a wise wife and mother.

# UNREQUITED LOVE

Love Jo all your days, if you choose, but don't let it spoil you, for it's wicked to throw away so many good gifts because you can't have the one you want. There, I won't lecture anymore . . .
    —Amy to Laurie.

# GIVING CREDIT

Amy's lecture did Laurie good, though, of course, he did not own it till long afterwards; men seldom do, for when women are the advisers, the lords of creation don't take the advice till they have persuaded themselves that it is just what they intended to do; then they act upon it, and, if it succeeds, they give the weaker vessel half the credit of it; if it fails,

they generously give her the whole.

Women work a good many miracles.

# MARRIAGE

Marriage is an excellent thing, after all. I wonder if I should blossom out half as well as you have, if I tried it?
    —Jo to Meg.

# LOVE

Honesty is the best policy in love as in law.

Jo and her professor cared little what anybody

thought, for they were enjoying the happy hour that seldom comes but once in any life, the magical moment which bestows youth on the old, beauty on the plain, wealth on the poor, and gives human hearts a foretaste of heaven.